To Elder Larkman

When you look at this book I hope you remember us and know me will always be Eternal Friends,

Happy Christmas 2002

The Stones
Bobbie, Andy, Luke
Florien Druckenthainer

Work Hard and ENJOY IT !!
Love + Best Wishes for
The remainder of your mission

Andrew Stone.

Elder Larkman

Remember the
spent with
you have
Chrissy, from the man.

James Stone. 02
xxoo
Haha

Matt 2 Nephi 3: 11-13

SPECTACULAR GOLD COAST & BRISBANE

SPECTACULAR GOLD COAST & BRISBANE

Grant Murray

NEW HOLLAND

First published in Australia in 2000 by
New Holland Publishers (Australia) Pty Ltd
Sydney • Auckland • London • Cape Town

14 Aquatic Drive Frenchs Forest NSW 2086 Australia
218 Lake Road Northcote Auckland New Zealand
24 Nutford Place London W1H 6DQ United Kingdom
80 McKenzie Street Cape Town 8001 South Africa

National Library of Australia Cataloguing-in-Publication Data:

Murray, Grant, 1963 –
Spectacular Gold Coast & Brisbane

ISBN 1 86436 531 5

1. Gold Coast (Qld.) — Pictorial works. 2. Brisbane (Qld.) — Pictorial works. I. Title.

919.432

Publishing Manager: Anouska Good
Editor: Marie-Claire Muir
Designer: Nanette Backhouse
Layout Artist: Karlman Roper
Reproduction: Colour Scan (Singapore)
Printer: Times (Malaysia)

Author photograph: Greg Teschner

To my dad and mum, Len and Merle, who shared with me the beauty of this magnificent country.

I would like to express my appreciation to my wife, Jacqueline, for her unending support during this project, and thanks to Greg Teschner for his support and technical advice. Thanks also to Leigh Zoubakin for sharing her knowledge of Brisbane.

CONTENTS

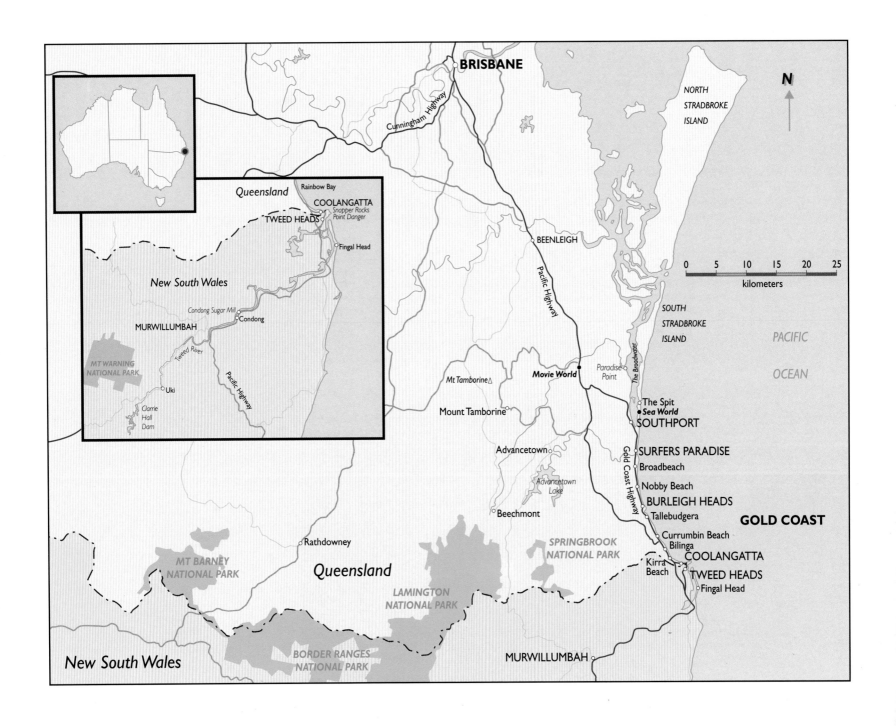

INTRODUCTION

Queensland's spectacular Gold Coast hosts an environment and lifestyle unlike any other in Australia. It enjoys a holiday atmosphere all year round and offers immediate access to many extraordinary natural landscapes. From the wide idyllic beaches and sparkling sea to the World Heritage rainforests of the mountains, the beauty of this region is unsurpassed.

Brisbane, Queensland's capital, lies just one hour north and offers all the excitement of a progressive, cosmopolitan city. With an easygoing outdoor lifestyle and a rich cultural heritage, it makes an ideal destination for visitors.

I live on the Gold Coast and the images in this book represent my own personal exploration of this unique region. I hope these images will inspire others to discover for themselves the rich diversity the Gold Coast offers.

GOLD COAST

The City of the Gold Coast is the name given to the stretch of land that runs from Coolangatta in the south to just beyond Southport, with Surfers Paradise, probably Australia's most famous seaside resort, in the middle. Situated an hour's drive south of Brisbane, this region is home to over 370,000 people and is Australia's seventh largest urban centre.

Exuding an energy unparalleled in Australia, the Gold Coast enjoys a holiday atmosphere throughout the year, and a celebration of one sort or another is never far away. Seaside cafes and markets, surf beaches and sheltered waterways, the family fun and excitement of theme parks and wildlife sanctuaries, colourful festivals, shopping extravaganzas and nightlife abound, offering never-ending entertainment. Complimented by an idyllic subtropical climate, with almost 300 sunny days a year, and a relaxed, leisure-orientated lifestyle, it is little wonder that the Gold Coast is Australia's favourite holiday playground, enticing over 4 million visitors each year.

Coolangatta's seaside markets allow locals to buy and sell their arts and crafts, or simply while away a sunny day, in a friendly, relaxed atmosphere.

A young girl plays her harp at the market, providing music for shoppers and stall-holders.

Coolangatta's beachside carnival, a traditional element of any seaside town, runs throughout the summer.

The movement and colour of the spinning carnival ride generate an excitement that beckons those seeking fun.

Brightly coloured boats with dragon heads and tails splash through the waters at Tweed Heads, Coolangatta's sister city on the New South Wales border. A traditional Chinese sport, dragon boat racing has become popular throughout much of coastal Australia.

The sun sets on Burleigh Heads, illuminating the evening sky over the mouth of Currumbin Creek.

A rockpool at Burleigh Heads reflects the dramatic colours of the sky as day breaks over Surfers Paradise in the distance.

A replica of Michelangelo's *David* towers over diners in the Raptis Plaza, Surfers Paradise.

Chess enthusiasts spend a sunny afternoon testing their skills against one another at Cavill Mall, Surfers Paradise.

A young clown prepares for the Tropicarnival street parade in Surfers Paradise. Held every year in October, the festival encompasses the whole of the Gold Coast and is the region's largest community event.

Meter Maids cruise the streets of the city on rollerblades and help out motorists by putting money in parking meters. Icons of Surfers Paradise, they too join the Tropicarnival parade.

During the annual kite festival at Surfers Paradise, the winds turn the sand and sky into a riot of bright colours.

The high-rises of Main Beach, north of Surfers Paradise, overlook the Pacific Ocean on one side, and the Nerang River on the other.

Clouds roll in from the ocean as the sun sets, casting a very different mood over Surfers Paradise and the Nerang River.

The Broadwater marina houses many of the pleasure craft and yachts that ply the waters during the day.

Dolphin Cove, at Sea World on The Broadwater, is the world's largest dolphin lagoon habitat.

The hair-raising Three Loop Corkscrew ride is one of the most popular rides at Sea World.

Warner Bros Movie World is a working studio combined with a fun park. Its streets are full of performers dressed as movie stars. Here, Marilyn Monroe dances in front of the Daily Planet.

The Police Academy Stunt Show is a popular Movie World attraction. Demonstrating how movie stunts are performed, it comes complete with car explosions, gun shots and endless thrills and spills from the stunt crew.

Fishing boats rest on The Broadwater at dusk, a reminder of the magnificent deep-sea fishing grounds of the Pacific Ocean lying beyond.

The fun and excitement of Surfers Paradise has crept north to centres like Main Beach, offering a cosmopolitan mix of restaurants, cafés, boutiques and galleries that overlook the magnificent Broadwater.

BEACH

Beaches are in a constant process of rejuvenation, constantly swept clean and reinvented by the relentless actions of waves and tides. They can also be a place of personal renewal, a place where one can spend quiet time absorbing the beach's mood and revelling in the diverse expressions of its character. Each day is a new creation, and it is exciting and surprising to see what each day brings.

The beach is a fundamental part of our Australian identity. It is from our beach culture that we draw so many of our national icons—the eternal vigilance of our bronzed lifesavers, the smell of sunscreen and salt air, the caress of sea spray on a face, the voluptuous curves of a dune, the tingle of effervescent surf on skin, beach umbrellas and sandcastles, hot sand squeaking beneath the feet. These images are ingrained in our collective consciousness—our lives would seem incomplete without them. It is hardly surprising, then, that the Gold Coast—offering the buzz of activity on the crowded city beaches or the solitude of untouched kilometres of dazzling white sand—is the focal point for the recreation of a nation.

An intense thunderstorm approaches Fingal Head on the far north coast of New South Wales. The historic lighthouse, built in 1878, is dwarfed by the enormous clouds that darken the sky.

As evening settles around Fingal Head, the lighthouse sends out its beacon to warn approaching vessels of the rocks below.

Waves sweep over the boulders below Point Danger, north of Fingal Head, as a thunderstorm approaches in the distance.

Pandanus palms stand silhouetted against the late afternoon sky as a wave surges toward Greenmount Beach, Coolangatta.

A beach patrol tower looks towards the lights of Coolangatta, an Aboriginal word meaning 'beautiful place'.

Families enjoy the relaxed atmosphere and sheltered waters of Coolangatta's Rainbow Bay.

Snapper Rocks is popular with anglers, who will often be up with the first light of day to enjoy the peace and quiet of the empty beach.

The sun rises through distant showers as waves surge over Snapper Rocks, Coolangatta.

Duranbah Beach at Tweed Heads is renowned for its 'break'. Here, surfers lie on their boards and wait for the next set.

As the sun rises, young board riders, intent on using every hour of daylight, hurry along the beach to join their friends in an impressive swell off Kirra Point, north of Coolangatta.

Early morning light swells above Kirra Point into a brilliant spectacle that is reflected in the glazed sands of Bilinga Beach.

Jagged rocks at Currumbin point across a calm sea towards Burleigh Heads, beyond which lies a string of relaxed coastal towns.

The long beaches of the Gold Coast provide perfect conditions for all manner of watersports. Here, the vibrant colours of catamaran sails fill the sky as the boats are prepared for a regatta at Currumbin Point.

Families enjoy the safe, protected waters of Tallebudgera Creek that adjoins the wind-sculpted slopes of Burleigh Head National Park.

Beach-goers enjoy the mid-winter sun on Burleigh Beach. The small national park on the steep headland, whose shore is lined with basalt boulders, is hemmed in by residential and tourist development.

Beach umbrellas litter the relatively quiet Burleigh Beach. In the distance lie the high-density high-rises of Surfers Paradise.

A familiar and reassuring site on most Australian beaches, the beach patrol keeps watch and ensures the safety of swimmers.

The red and yellow flags signify the strip of water guarded by the beach patrol. 'Stay between the flags' is a refrain well-known to beach-goers.

Sun-worshippers are lured to Gold Coast beaches throughout the year in pursuit of their ultimate goal, the perfect tan.

There is plenty of room on the beaches for both surfers and swimmers, but to prevent accidents, each must stay in their separate areas.

Beachside showers exist on most beaches, allowing swimmers to remove sand and salt after a dip in the surf.

Born of a lifesaving tradition that began in the early 1900s, the first of its kind in the world, the surf lifesaver is an icon of Australian culture. Here, a group of them pose during a break in a surf carnival at Burleigh Beach.

On many beaches the wooden surfboats used for rescuing distressed swimmers have been replaced by motorised dinghies, but the traditional craft are still used in competitions which are held along the coast throughout the summer.

Surf lifesavers stand poised in anticipation of the starting whistle in a race at Burleigh Beach.

A young girl waits for a breaking wave before joining her family in the surf.

Waves crash on Nobby Beach during the early hours of morning.

Subtle morning light and a warm breeze make the Spit, north of Southport, an enjoyable place to start the day.

The light of dawn gathers over the Broadwater as boats at Paradise Point are stranded on the shore by the receding tide.

HINTERLAND

For many, the Gold Coast's greatest attraction lies in its remarkable hinterland. Pristine mountain rainforests provide sanctuary from the often frenetic pace of the coast, deep gorges and spectacular escarpments shelter tumbling waterfalls, country roads wind through canefields and broad rivers meander to the sea. Scenic rural villages, markets and festivals all convey something of the vibrancy of a region that has captured the hearts of so many.

The dramatic mountain landscape of the Gold Coast was formed by volcanic action over 23 million years ago which resulted in the largest shield volcano in the southern hemisphere, Mount Warning (1,157 metres), which covers more than 5,000 square kilometres. So named by Captain Cook to warn mariners of dangerous reefs, Mount Warning is one of the first points of the Australian mainland to be touched by the sun each morning.

Within the sheltering forests of the region's enormous World Heritage listed national parks hides a world filled with all the enchantment and wonder of a fairytale—a world in which glistening fern glades and antarctic beech forest are cloaked in mist, and where moss-laden branches embrace over merrily chuckling streams. These sanctuaries provide a unique opportunity to experience the region's natural heritage.

Mount Warning stands guard over canefields near Murwillumbah and is reflected in a tributary of the Tweed River.

Sunset reflects on Clarrie Hall Dam near Uki, a small township that lies on the edge of Mount Warning National Park.

The sugarcane strip that provides Queensland's most important crop begins in northern New South Wales. Each year during the harvest season, between July and December, cane fires set the evening skies in the Tweed Valley ablaze.

The sugar processing mill at Condong is the only one in the Tweed Valley. It represents a major industry and source of income in the area.

This rustic general store lies across the road from the Condong sugar mill.

'Lisnagar', a classic Queensland-style homestead near Murwillumbah, was a stop for Cobb & Co. coaches during the early 1900s.

Known for its lush canefields, farmlands and tropical fruit plantations, the natural abundance of the Tweed Valley is celebrated at the Tweed Banana Festival, held annually at Murwillumbah. Here, street performers entertain passers-by.

Banana Jim, mascot of the festival, leads a street parade.

Late afternoon sun warms the verdant rolling hills of Beechmont, north of Lamington and Springbrook national parks.

An old milk shed stands alone in a field near Beechmont, a reminder of the hinterland's rich agricultural heritage.

The sun sets through bushfire smoke as lightning from an approaching thunderstorm strikes the land.

Subtle evening tones of pink and mauve colour the still waters of Advancetown Lake, north-east of Beechmont.

Water plunges through the eroded basalt roof into a cavern at the Natural Bridge section of Springbrook National Park.

The sun rises over farmland near Lamington National Park, 20 000 hectares of mountainous terrain that was formed some 23 million years ago when the area was alive with volcanic activity.

Chalahn Falls cascade over volcanic rocks in Lamington National Park, home to Australia's largest preserved stand of subtropical rainforest.

Water tumbles over lichen-encrusted boulders along West Canungra Creek.

Early morning light dapples the forest floor on Snake Ridge, Lamington National Park.

Fungi, ferns and mosses flourish in the cool, moist environment below the canopy of Lamington's rainforests.

Morning light illuminates a stand of Piccabeen Palms in the Palm Grove section of Mount Tambourine National Park.

The buttressed roots of a rainforest tree cling tenaciously to the forest floor in Palm Grove.

An old farm shed stands beneath the rugged heights of Mount Barney National Park, near Rathdowney.

Mount Barney's craggy slopes dominate the landscape of the surrounding farms and grazing land.

The sun sets over Border Ranges National Park on the Queensland–New South Wales border.

The Border Ranges is a place of extreme diversity and luxurience. The high number of plants that grow here and nowhere else make it an important area for floral conservation, one of the reasons for its World Heritage listing.

A tranquil pool at Brindle Creek, crowded by cool temperate rainforest, provides relief from the summer heat.

A tumbled mass of lichen-covered boulders surrounds the base of a rainforest tree near the top of Burleigh Head National Park.

BRISBANE

Brisbane, the capital of Queensland (also known as 'the Sunshine State'), has a population of over one million people and is Australia's third largest city. Situated in the beautiful south-east, only one hour north of the Gold Coast, Brisbane offers all the excitement of a progressive, cosmopolitan city, with an easygoing outdoor lifestyle and an enviable climate of hot summers and clear, mild winters.

The heart of Brisbane is intimately entwined in the broad meandering arms of the Brisbane River, which provides a focal point for the city's recreational and cultural activities. Riverside walkways, the inner-city beach at South Bank, museums and galleries, art and craft markets, colourful parklands and historic buildings, all convey a sense of the uniqueness of this beautiful subtropical city.

Spanning the Brisbane River, the Story Bridge is the gateway to the city and links Kangaroo Point to New Farm. Designed by J C Bradfield (who also designed the Sydney Harbour Bridge), this landmark bridge was built in 1940.

The heritage-listed Treasury Building was built in the 1880s and is considered a masterpiece of mid-Victorian Renaissance design. After renovations to the cost of $330 million, it reopened in 1995 as Conrad Treasury Casino.

The magnificent Edwardian Lands Administration Building has been restored and reinvented as the Hotel Conrad. One of Brisbane's finest hotels, it is steeped in political history.

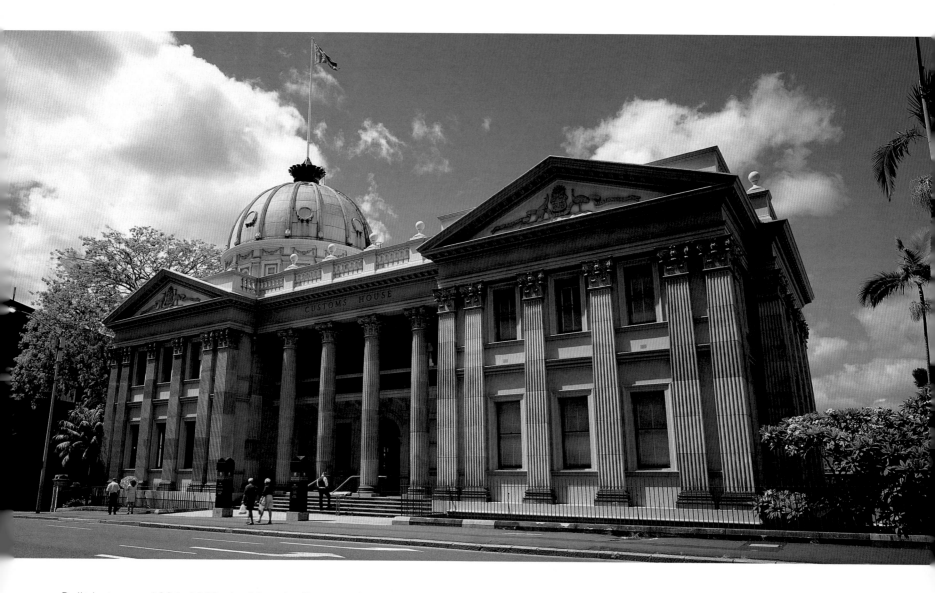

Built between 1886–1889, the historic Customs House, crowned with a massive copper dome, is one of Brisbane's most impressive landmarks and reflects the grand nature of much of the city's architecture.

The Windmill is Brisbane's oldest building. Built by convicts in 1828, it was used to grind the flour and maize meal for the penal settlement.

New Farm Park, on the banks of the Brisbane River, is an oasis of jacaranda trees and rose gardens. Often on Sunday afternoons music recitals are held in the bandstand. It is also a popular spot for weddings and christenings.

Cascades in the forecourt of the Performing Arts Complex hush the sounds of the city. Part of the Queensland Cultural Centre, the complex is home to the Lyric Theatre, Concert Hall and Cremorne Studio Theatre.

A hot air balloon glides high over the Brisbane River.

The Entrance Court, a short walk from the heritage-listed South Brisbane Station, marks the beginning of the 40-acres of riverside parkland and entertainment areas that make up South Bank, formerly the site of Brisbane's World Expo '88.

A street performer entertains a crowd at South Bank.

Tourists and locals alike escape Brisbane's summer heat in South Bank's inner-city man-made beach.

Children play on stepping stones at South Bank Parklands.

Holiday-makers enjoy a lazy summer afternoon.

Street performers contribute to the festive atmosphere.

A Moreton Bay Fig leans over the Brisbane River at Kangaroo Point in the last light of day.

Sculptures adorn the picnic areas and walkways of Kangaroo Point. Many came from the Brisbane World Expo '88, others were commissioned specifically for the area by Brisbane City Council.

The 6.5–tonne 'Fossil Fish' sculpture, by well-known Brisbane artist Christopher Trotter, stands on the riverside pathway.

Located on the banks of the Brisbane River, the beautiful City Botanic Gardens offer a peaceful respite from the central business district.

Jacaranda flowers carpet the Botanic Gardens throughout October.

Waterlilies adorn the fountain in the Botanic Gardens.

Colourful flower stalls add vibrancy to the Riverside Markets.

A soothing quiet falls over the Brisbane River as night descends.

Fireworks explode over the city of Brisbane on 26 January, in celebration of Australia Day.